Adventures with

Flint

The Fabulous Pomeranian

Published by Willow Creek Press, Inc.
P.O. Box 147, Minocqua, Wisconsin 54548

All Photos © Robin Yu

Design: Donnie Rubo & Sara Olson
Printed in China

Adventures with Flint

The Fabulous Pomeranian

By Robin Yu

▣ WILLOW CREEK PRESS®

My Memoir

Food Critic. Vacuum Understudy. Lap Warmer. Fluffy Model. Author.

Hi everyone! It's me, Flint! I may be getting cuter every day, but I'm not getting any younger. That's why I decided to sit down to write this memoir about my fabulous adventures over the last year. It was a challenge, but luckily I finished my rewrites just before running out of paper. Whether I'm swimming under the sea, caught in a bubble explosion or romping through the tulip patch, you never know where my four tiny feet will take me. Hope you enjoy these memories as much as I did making them!

Let's get this New Year's party started.
Starting the New Year off right!

Do you know what time it is? It's tickle time!
And hugs! I love hugs!

Ahh, Valentine's Day. My favorite holiday where love is everywhere!

Love is so delicious! I love LOVE!

Lip smacking good! Now all I need is some peanut butter!

Jelly kisses for you!

I'm a Pom on a ledge with cabin fever.
Quick, cuddle me or I'll jump!

This snow stuff is serious business. I think I'm ready for spring!

Maybe I'll just nap till spring arrives.

Never mind. I'm too excited.

Rain...

Sometimes I like it...

And sometimes...

I don't!

Woohoo, Spring is finally here! Are you ready for your close-up?

It's a hard day's work, but somebody's gotta do it. Spring cleaning at its cutest!

I don't care what anyone says. This is definitely the most efficient way to clean a bowl.

What do you mean? Playing in clean laundry doesn't count as helping?

Will you be my pen pal?
Keeping up with my fan mail is one of my favorite parts of the day!

It's best to meditate in a place where you feel completely relaxed...

...ZZZZZZ

Is this how big dogs are made? If so, keep it coming!

Tiptoeing through the tulips?

How about we DANCE through the tulips!

Thinking about places to hide those Easter eggs.
Hippity hop hop, hippity hop!

Look Mom, I'm a Peep! Sweet, soft and colorful.

The secret to gardening is to be involved...

...VERY involved.

Looking forward to summer and watermelon agility!

Bouncing and POUNCING!

1, 2, 3...

...JUMP!

Sometimes you need a little citrus spritzing!

Light and refreshing, just like me.

Ahoy there, little duckie!

Goldfish and me, under the sea.

Good to be back on dry land!

Time for a snooze in the tall, sweet grass. Maybe I'll dream about...

Treasure hunts...

BUBBLE EXPLOSIONS...

...and The Land of Milk and Cookies!

The heart "nose" what it wants...
and it's telling me it wants this strawberry!

And the best way to enjoy a strawberry is when it's in the form of ice cream.

It's a fruity, juicy, candy storm!

Sometimes you gotta put your feet up and take a break!

Little dog, big forest.
Don't miss the Pom for the trees!

Summer brings out the rosy glow in my smile.

They smell like flowers, but they look like cotton candy! Do I eat them or not?

Yellow might just be my favorite color…

Let's go on a field trip!

What's better than a day at the beach?

Wait for me!

Do you like my hair? I just give it a shake and off I go!

These apples look pretty good!

Let's take a closer look!

Smile!
Where's my smile? Right underneath my little nose!

Blowing in the wind! Except not me, of course. I weigh just a bit more than these leaves!

Trying out some of my best costumes for Halloween! Tricks and treats are the best!

RAWR!

WOW!

Open wide! It's snowing marshmallows!

It's my very own winter wonderland!

This balancing thing isn't as easy as it looks.

This year has been such a tasty treat! Can't wait to do it again next year...

Many thanks to all my friends and fans around the world!
If you would like to follow me on my adventures, use
the QR code below or visit www.flintthepomeranian.com.